The True Wesleyan

by Ken Schenck

Copyright © 2012 Kenneth Schenck

All Rights Reserved

ISBN-13: 978-1479247844
ISBN-10: 1479247847

All Scripture quotations, unless otherwise indicated, are taken from the *New Revised Standard Version Bible*, copyright © 1989 National Council of the Churches of Christ in the United States of America. Used by permission. All rights reserved.

Contents

1. The True Wesleyan — 7
2. A Generous Tradition — 9
3. A Heart-Oriented Tradition — 12
4. God Is Love — 16
5. The Cross as Love — 20
6. Human Freedom — 23
7. Optimistic about Love — 25
8. Loving the Whole Person — 29
9. Loving into Social Structures — 33
10. The Importance of Faithfulness — 37
11. Scripture as Sacrament — 42
12. Looking Ahead — 47

1. "True" Wesleyan?

In 1843, a Methodist named Orange Scott started a publication called *The True Wesleyan*. That was also the year that he and a number of other Methodists split off from the Methodist Episcopal Church over its failure to take a position against slavery. Those who were at the founding convention of the "Wesleyan Methodist Connection" in Utica, New York, believed that if John Wesley, the founder of Methodism, were still alive, theirs was the kind of Methodism he would endorse.[1]

They were probably right. Not only did they have Wesley's position on slavery, but they also had a less "top down" form of government that Wesley would have liked. There are lots of Methodists around today: United Methodists, Free Methodists, Wesleyans, Nazarenes, to name a few. I wouldn't want to say that any one of them preserves the "true" John Wesley. In fact, why would we want to consider Wesley himself as some sort of an absolute or timeless model? After all, he was a child of the 1700s, and surely among his heirs are some improvements somewhere on the original model!

Nevertheless, I choose the old title, "true Wesleyan," because I believe there is an incredible richness to the Wesleyan tradition. I believe that the

Wesleyan tradition has a lot to offer to the church of the twenty-first century. As the very first point below shows, part of this offering is its very "catholicity." One of the distinctives of the Wesleyan tradition is its willingness to include and find the good in other traditions.

So the intention of this small book is not to exclude or boast but to present some offerings that might be attractive not only to others, but to those in the Wesleyan tradition who may have lost sight of its own richness. It is in that spirit that we embark on this quest for the best of the Wesleyan tradition.

2. A Generous Tradition

Surely every Christian tradition has something to contribute to the body of Christ. We can appreciate the sense of security in God that Baptist traditions have. We can appreciate the emphasis on grace and freedom in the Lutheran tradition. We can appreciate the depth of the Roman Catholic tradition. Surely no Christian tradition has everything right, and surely we can agree on many things in almost all Christian traditions.

The Wesleyan tradition also has something to contribute, a tradition that traces its origins ultimately back to an eighteenth century Anglican minister named John Wesley. We would not think for one moment that we have everything figured out. Indeed, like almost all Christian traditions in North America, the Wesleyan tradition today includes numerous little groups that spun off from their original Methodist roots, each with its own unique history.

In the current climate, you would not have to pick a "denomination," a group of churches that join together on the basis of some commonality. In fact, some churches have banded together on the common ground of opposition to denominationalism itself. The current climate also includes a multitude of non-denominational churches, and the house church movement is also going strong.

At the same time, a quick look at the beliefs and practices of any non-denominational church will almost always reveal the influence of historical Christian traditions. How do they baptize? What do they believe about particular issues? The answers to these questions almost always reflect the influence of particular Christian traditions. Among these streams of Christian tradition, the Wesleyan tradition is surely an attractive one.

One reason is because the Wesleyan tradition is by its very nature already generous toward groups with differing ideas and practices. This is because it is a heart-oriented tradition that focuses primarily on our intentions and character. It is not that the Wesleyan tradition is unconcerned with ideas or has no interest in the pursuit of knowledge. It is only that its focus on virtue and pure intentions make those concerns a second or even third order of business.

John Wesley, like most great thinkers, has left us with several memorable statements that capture the key values of his tradition. One such statement was that "if your heart is as my heart, then put your hand in mind." Thus we find that the Wesleyan tradition is a *generous* tradition toward others. When we are at our best, we are more about finding what we have in common with others than with separating from others because of our differences.

Indeed, because of this heart-orientation,

> The Wesleyan tradition is a generous tradition. As Wesley once said, "If your heart is as my heart, then put your hand in mine."

many, although not all churches in the Wesleyan tradition have developed a great freedom in church practice. For example, you will find almost every form of baptism in my own denomination, everything from believer's baptism to infant baptism to no baptism at all. While I have my own preferences, I delight in a tradition that does not fight over baptism, communion, or so many of the Christian practices that have so often divided churches.

The Wesleyan tradition at its best is a generous tradition toward other traditions, captured well in Wesley's sermon, "On a Catholic Spirit." Generosity in this sense is not the same as thinking all beliefs and practices are equally valid. It is simply an orientation toward others that sees the most important common ground as a matter of our intentions and character, not whether we all think and act the same way.

3. A Heart-Oriented Tradition

Is it possible that a person's "head" could be wrong on very many things, and yet that person be right with God? By the same token, could a person have all the right beliefs and yet be as far away from God as the most violent criminal? The best of the Wesleyan tradition says "yes." In a different context, 1 Samuel 16:7 puts it memorably: "the LORD does not see as mortals see; they look on the outward appearance, but the LORD looks on the heart" (NRSV).

We can put it another way. Could a person "mess up" in very many ways for various reasons, and yet that person be right with God? Similarly, could a person's outward actions appear virtuous and honorable and yet her heart be far from God? The best of the Wesleyan tradition says "yes." God is able to divide "soul from spirit" and to "judge the thoughts and intentions of the heart" (Heb. 4:12).

Let's go even one step further. Could it be possible that some people, perhaps those born in lands far from Christianity, have nonetheless responded appropriately to God "according to the light they have"? Is it possible to know almost nothing about God, perhaps never even heard of

Jesus' name, and yet respond to the direct call of God in your heart?[2] While we must be very careful about this sort of speculation, it fits with the Wesleyan tradition and Wesley's notion of prevenient grace that finds us before we even realize God is calling us.

A sense of the heart as the focal point of God's concern, more than your ideas or actions, reflects the Pietist influence on Wesley and, of course, ultimately traces its origins to Scripture. Beliefs were certainly important to Wesley, and actions were even more important to Wesley than your beliefs. But the best of the Wesleyan tradition has always recognized that, for me as an individual, my heart is God's focal concern. "It is what comes out of a person that defiles. For it is from within, from the human heart, that evil intentions come" (Mark 7:20-21, NRSV).

This heart orientation manifested itself in Wesley's definition of sin as a "voluntary transgression of the law." Is it possible to sin unintentionally? Certainly it is—we can *wrong* others without meaning to do so. We can also *do wrong* without even realizing it. It is not incorrect to call such wrongdoing "sin," because it is this sort of sin that is the primary interest of the Levitical law. By contrast, the Levitical law gives little hope for atonement in the case of "high handed," intentional sins (cf. Num. 15).

> "God looks on the heart." God receives us based on how we respond to "the light we have" and sin as it matters to him is when we knowingly and intentionally do wrong.

On the other hand, the New Testament says almost

nothing about unintentional sin. And it would be quite mistaken to think that God's standard for sin in the New Testament is absolute perfection. Paul came closest to giving us a New Testament definition when he said that "whatever does not proceed from faith is sin" (Rom. 14:23, NRSV). This is the standard God has set for our relationship with him. It is not, "whoever does not believe the right things has sinned." It is not even "whoever does not do the right things has sinned." It is "the one whose thoughts and actions come from the wrong motivations has sinned."

Some Christian traditions have struggled more than others with the postmodern challenge of these last decades. The postmodern critique pointed out how ambiguous language can be. The postmodern critique pointed out how often politics and power are involved in what we call truth. The postmodern critique exposed how unaware we often are of the cultural and historical influences on our paradigms for understanding reality, and how paradigms tend to change over time. We can learn from these critiques without abandoning our confidence that truth exists.

Indeed, somewhat ironically, the postmodern critique has actually reinforced the theological values the Wesleyan tradition has always had. We have always known the limitations of knowledge, even when it comes in Christian garb. Wesley was certainly a thinker, but he was also a pragmatist, the direction in which the postmodern critique pushes us. And our emphasis on transformation and divine encounter is completely unaffected. The best of the Wesleyan tradition has always known that truth is far more a matter of what is going on deep inside us than the relatively superficial thoughts we have with our conscious minds.

4. God Is Love

What we have been expressing is the way God relates to his creation, a creation that is alienated from him in its knowledge and being. When we look to Scripture to tell us about what God is like, we find a number of pictures. God is love. God is just. When we ask what God's dominant mode of operation toward the creation is, surely love is the dominant characteristic.

John 3:16 captures this characteristic well. God's love stands behind his sending of Jesus into the world so that *anyone* might be reconciled to him. Wesleyans do not believe that God has only chosen a select a few to rescue, seemingly arbitrarily. John Wesley himself taught that God had a "prevenient" grace that empowered us to move toward God long before we even know God is at work. It is a grace that "goes ahead" of us, indeed, that was in action in some respects before God created the world.

The way we think about God has massive implications. For example, we have already mentioned the possibility that God might judge humanity "according to the light we have," rather than against an absolute standard. The end result is that we may find individuals in the kingdom of God who had never heard the name of Jesus while they were alive but who had responded appropriately to the prevenient light God had brought to them.

At the same time, it is not clear that God extends this light to us indefinitely. Perhaps we best take what the Bible calls the "hardening of the heart" as a rejection of God's light to the point that God abandons a person to his or her own destructive path. And however we might understand eternal condemnation, it surely represents a path set by our own rejection of God's advances, resulting in a permanent separation from him that reflects our own hardened identity.

Some Christian traditions do not think

> God in his authority has every right to empower free will in humanity if he wants to do so.

God could have complete authority and be "sovereign" if humans could disobey or defy him. But the Wesleyan tradition believes that God in his authority has every right to empower free will in humanity if he wants to do so. The best of the Wesleyan tradition does not operate from a sense of God enraged by our destructive actions. This is one picture we find in the Bible, but all such pictures are given to help us grasp a God who is beyond our understanding. The more important and dominant picture in the New Testament is of a God grieved by our self-destructive patterns.

Again, the Wesleyan way of understanding God has implications that fit with what we find in the biblical witness. For example, while some Christian groups emphasize ethical absolutes, the best of the Wesleyan tradition emphasizes a priority of values and the importance of exceptions. By definition, an absolute has no exceptions. If you believe that keeping the Sabbath is an absolute, then you believe there is no circumstance in which it would be right *not* to keep the Sabbath.

Wesleyans, as all Christians, do indeed believe in the two great absolutes that Jesus reiterated from the Old Testament: love God and love neighbor (e.g., Matt. 22:36-40). There is no situation that could ever arise when it would be appropriate to make an exception to these two principles. But the ethic of both Jesus and Paul focused on making exceptions to the "Law" when a higher value was at stake. People trump rules for their own sake.

Jesus does not come into conflict with religious leaders in Mark 2 because of his absolutism. On the contrary, it is his opponents who take an absolutist perspective on the Sabbath. Paul did not come into conflict with other Christians because of his absolutism, but because he set aside parts of the Law that were hindering the gospel. The normal level of Christian ethics is universal in scope, but not absolute in practice.

The Parable of the Good Samaritan captures this principle well. In this story, the Levite and priest ignore the love of their neighbor because of the purity standards of Leviticus. By contrast, the picture we get of God's character—and of his ideal for us—is of a love that prizes people over rules. Jesus never agrees with the Samaritan over theology and practice. He just demonstrates that such things do not trump the love of one's "enemy." The best of the Wesleyan tradition sees God in these terms and believes that in his relationship to humanity, "mercy triumphs over judgment" (Jas. 2:13).

5. The Cross as Love

When we say that God is just, we are saying there is a certain order to things. God gives us freedom to choose our path, but some paths are destructive to ourselves and others. God's justice is his protection of others, his attempt to steer us in the right direction, and at times, his abandonment of us to our own self-destructive freedom. It is more "formative" than "summative." Its primary goal is to shape us (to form us, help us do better on the test next time) more than to punish us (like a final grade that is simply a response to what we've done). It is discipline and training for the next time more than punishment in the thirst for justice.

> God's discipline is primarily formative, to shape us, rather than summative or punitive.

Some Christian traditions primarily emphasize God's justice as punitive, as penalty for offending God himself. Their sense is that someone must pay when God's sovereignty has been undermined. The best of the Wesleyan tradition questions the mechanical tone of this logic.[3] For example, it is not the logic of the Parable of the Prodigal Son in Luke 15, where the father has the authority simply to forgive his wayward son. It is not the logic of the Parable of the Unforgiving Servant in Matthew 18, where the master has the authority simply to write off the servant's debt with no repayment whatsoever. It is not the message of the prophets in Isaiah, Jeremiah, or Micah, who argue that God is ultimately uninterested in their countless animal sacrifices.

The cross does satisfy the order of things. It is the ultimate embodiment of the cost of human freedom gone amok. It embodies the pain of our alienation from God. It is the most powerful picture of God's justice. It is the consummate embodiment of one stream of biblical pictures about God and humanity.

Could God, for his part, have reconciled humanity simply by his divine command? The parables and prophets say yes, which ultimately makes the cross even more an embodiment of his love than his justice. The cross is God making a choice to reconcile humanity. The cross is God showing his willingness to identify with us, to enter into our pain and alienation. The cross is God's invitation to us. These are not the only valid pictures of the cross, but they are the ones most significant for the best of the Wesleyan tradition.

The cross is God's love, his reaching out to us. "Rarely will anyone die for a righteous person—though perhaps for a good person someone might actually dare to die. But God proves his love for us in that while we still were sinners Christ died for us" (Rom. 5:7-8, NRSV).

At the same time, make no mistake, the Wesleyan tradition, along with historic Christianity, recognizes that God has chosen Christ—his incarnation, death, resurrection—as the only path for reconciliation. The Wesleyan tradition might question how much a person must *know* about what God has done through Christ to be reconciled. But the Wesleyan tradition affirms with historic Christendom that Christ is the only way.

6. Human Freedom

You can see how central human freedom is to a Wesleyan view of the world. To be sure, Wesley did not believe in anything like absolute free will, where we have complete control over what we want and do. Wesley believed that our ability to make moral choices was a gift from God, empowered by God's prevenient grace, a grace that finds us when we are not seeking it.

Indeed, if we have a spark of free will inside, it must surely be a miracle. The more we understand the brain and human psychology, the more we realize the extent to which "who we are" is a function of the physical structure and chemistry of our brain, the harder the idea of human freedom becomes. The debate has even moved beyond whether our actions are determined or free. Quantum physics has raised the question of whether they are in fact completely undetermined—random, chaotic, and unpredictable.

At the same time, more than Wesleyan thinking is at stake. The greatest objection to the truth of Christianity is the problem of evil, why God allows evil to continue in the world. The best answer, although it is not perfect, is that a world in which people have freedom to make moral choices is a better world than one in which they do not. Christian traditions that do not believe in human freedom run the risk either of making God the direct author of evil or making him unjust himself, views which seem to render Christianity incoherent.

The belief that God has created a world where humans are free to follow or not follow him has implications for the way we live. The Wesleyan tradition, when it is consistent with itself, is thus not oriented around forcing others to conform to Christian values. To be sure, it has always been active in stopping the oppression of others. But it is not like other traditions that view wrongdoing primarily through the lens of offending God. It does not try to legislate Christian morality beyond the protection of others. Its prophetic voice to those outside the church is more *for* others than *against* sin.

We thus relate to others in a different

> The Wesleyan sense of a prophetic voice is more *for* others than *against* sin, since God himself allows humans to make bad choices.

way. The parent does not get enraged because the child has disobeyed, an effrontery to authority. The parent is concerned for what the child will become, and disciplines to try to steer the will of the child in the right direction. Discipline is formative not summative. It is about formation more than about punishment. The best of the Wesleyan tradition will thus live out its sense of God empowered human freedom from a motivation of love.

7. Optimistic about Love

Love of our neighbor is the primary way in which we demonstrate the love of God in our lives. Love of neighbor includes love of all people. Jesus in the Sermon and the Mount and his parables commanded not only love of our neighbor but love of our enemy. He left no one that we are not obligated to love.

The Wesleyan tradition is not unique in coming to these conclusions. This is the *Christian* understanding of ethics. You cannot legitimately justify hatred toward people in any Christian tradition on any basis. Those who hide behind Christianity to justify hatred of others are thus at best fooling themselves, at worst they are condemning themselves.

People who call themselves Christians—as those of other religions—have often pretended that Christianity justified their hatred of other races and people groups. They have wanted to obliterate nations or destroy Muslims in God's name. They have put others to death because they disagreed theologically. They have lynched African-Americans and beaten homosexuals. They have resisted giving women and African-Americans equal rights, they have justified hatred toward illegal immigrants in the name of punishing law-breakers. It is not the Wesleyan tradition but Christ who indicts these attitudes pretending to be Christian.

So the Wesleyan tradition is not unique in its affirmation of love as the fulfillment of all God's ethical requirements of humanity. Where the Wesleyan tradition has been unique is in its optimism about the extent to which God wants to empower us to love. Other traditions rightly affirm love as the fulfillment of God's law, but they are not optimistic about the possibility of achieving God's standard. By contrast, John Wesley was bold enough to speak of "perfect love" as what God wants to equip us to do.

God has not set a standard for us that we cannot meet, or as 1 Corinthians 10:13 puts it, "No testing has overtaken you that is not common to everyone. God is faithful, and he will not let you be tested beyond your strength, but with the testing he will also provide the way out so that you may be able to endure it" (NRSV). Failure in loving God and your neighbor should not and cannot be our default expectation. God does not expect "perfection" in any absolute sense. As we mentioned above, the standard for measuring sin in the New Testament is not absolute perfection. The standard is our basic intent, amid all the conflicting impulses that are part and parcel of the human brain.

> We believe that, by God's power, a person might go the rest of her life without intentionally doing something blatantly wrong.

Here is a point of some distinctiveness

among Christian traditions. Wesleyans do not believe that sin is the default state of the believer. In theory, we believe that a person might, by God's power, go the whole rest of her life without intentionally choosing to do wrong. We are, again, not talking about the eddies and currents of human intent. We are talking about a clear cut choice: I know God wants me to do A, but I am tempted to do B. The Wesleyan tradition is optimistic about the power of the Spirit to consistently empower you to choose A, even without fail for the rest of your life. Indeed, we believe God can change you to where you do the loving thing with great delight.

It is a great time for the Wesleyan tradition in terms of biblical interpretation. Most scholars now—even from traditions that believe differently—acknowledge that Paul was not talking about his *current* struggle with sin in Romans 7. You would have to rip that chapter from its context to argue that Paul was saying he could not help but sin *today*. The entire flow from Romans 6-8 is about how God's grace does *not* justify a life of sin, where love defines the standard (Rom. 13:10). Most now have come to recognize that Paul is putting himself in the shoes of someone who wants to do good but does not have the Spirit's power to do it.

The rediscovery of Paul's Jewish context has drawn our attention not only to his optimism about keeping the Law before he believed on Christ (e.g., Phil. 3:6) but also his optimism about being morally blameless after he believed (e.g., Phil. 1:10-11). Romans 8 transcends the hopeless situation of

Romans 7, so that "the just requirement of the law might be fulfilled in us, who walk not according to the flesh but according to the Spirit" (8:4, NRSV). "Walking" is about living, not some theoretical fulfillment in Christ that does not show up in our own lives. As Paul puts it in Galatians 5:16, "walk by the Spirit, and you will not carry out the desire of the flesh" (NASB).

This is perhaps the most distinctive aspect of the Wesleyan tradition, its optimism about the level of love that God wants to enable us to have in this life. The rediscovery of Paul's Jewish context has freed us up to see loving intent not only as God's standard of righteousness. It has freed us to see love as an attainable standard through the power of the Holy Spirit.

8. Loving the Whole Person

The Wesleyan tradition would not be unique in believing that love of our neighbors must go beyond an invitation to believe on Christ to reach into every area of life. The idea of reaching out to those in need—the poor, the widow, the orphan—is a dominant theme of the Bible, and cannot legitimately be placed in competition with the call to evangelism as we now define it.[4] The Bible from the Old Testament to Jesus to the rest of the New Testament pushes us to do both. Indeed, few will respond or consider the good news to be good news, if it comes as mere words without any demonstration of real love.

The idea of "social justice" originates in the Bible. When Job is describing his righteousness before God he describes it this way: "I delivered the poor who cried, and the orphan who had no helper. The blessing of the wretched came upon me, and I caused the widow's heart to sing for joy. I put on righteousness, and it clothed me; my justice was like a robe and a turban. I was eyes to the blind, and feet to the lame. I was a father to the needy, and I championed the cause of the stranger" (Job 29:12-17, NRSV). Job describes his righteousness, his *justice*, in terms of reaching out to the material needs of others.

This core value of Israel reaches from the Law to the Prophets to the Writings. In the Law, Israel is to leave food in its fields for the poor and the immigrant (Lev. 19:1-2). When we look to the Prophets, we find that the theme of social injustice is a dominant concern, as much as any indictment of Israel for breaking its covenant with God. Isaiah 10 condemns a government that makes "iniquitous decrees, who write oppressive statutes, to turn aside the needy from justice and to rob the poor of my people of their right, that widows may be your spoil, and that you may make the orphans your prey" (10:1-2, NRSV).

In the Gospel of Luke, the theme of Jesus' earthly ministry is to "bring good news to the poor. He has sent me to proclaim release to the captives and recovery of sight to the blind, to let the oppressed go free, to proclaim the year of the Lord's favor" (4:18-19, NRSV). Jesus is quoting Isaiah 61 as a kind of inaugural address for his ministry, and concern for the disempowered is a dominant theme of the two volumes of Luke and Acts. In Matthew 25, helping those with material needs is the *only* criteria mentioned by which God assigns individuals their eternal destiny.

Certainly when we apply this core biblical

> Concern for the poor and the oppressed is not only a core value of the Wesleyan tradition; it is a core biblical value that appears throughout all Scripture.

value to today, we must take into account our differing circumstances. The situation of the poor today is not the same as the situation of the biblical poor. As with all application of Scripture, we must take the general principles and apply them with a view to the points of continuity and discontinuity. But there is no denying the principle. Loving our neighbor in every dimension of life is a core biblical and Christian value. Indeed, these sorts of things stand at the very heart of what it means to love our neighbor. As 1 John 3:17 says, "How does God's love abide in anyone who has the world's goods and sees a brother or sister in need and yet refuses help?" (NRSV), and this love extends beyond the Christian family (e.g., Gal. 6:10).

Again, the Wesleyan tradition is not unique in recognizing this core Christian value. John Wesley himself left the normal confines of the church to preach to coal-miners and others who were disempowered in the English society of the day. Many believe that the love he showed to the lower classes was one of the reasons England did not have the bloody revolution that France did at the end of the 1700s. He was part of the wave of empowerment that ended with the abolition of slavery and the enactment of child-labor laws in England.

The Wesleyan tradition at its best has followed Wesley's example. For example, it is no coincidence that the Salvation Army is a church in the Wesleyan tradition. It is a church whose concern for the material needs of others is so clear that many do not even realize that it is a denomination.

Churches in the Wesleyan tradition have regularly kept a food pantry for the needy who might stop by. Concern for those in need is thus a core Wesleyan value, just as it is a core Christian value.

It is unfortunate that the early twentieth century pushed so many grass roots Christians away from this core Christian value. At that time, conservative Christians distinguished themselves from what was called the "social gospel." Those who advocated a social gospel at that time did not believe in things like the deity or resurrection of Christ.

But the fundamentalists who reacted to them threw out half of the gospel in their reaction. The modernists' concern for the poor and needy was *all that was left* of their Christianity, not a sign of their opposition to historic Christian values. It was perfectly appropriate for the fundamentalists to reject their disbelief of core items of Christian faith. But in rejecting their concern for the poor, the fundamentalists themselves rejected core items of Christian faith. The Wesleyan tradition in its core values rejects this strand within American conservatism.

9. Loving into Social Structures

God has done an amazing thing these last few hundred years. We have witnessed the working of the love principle beyond the individual into the very fabric of society, into societal structures. In Western society, we have seen a leveling in which the least in society have risen to have a say in their destiny. We have seen the abolition of slavery and the empowerment of women to vote and set their own courses. From time to time the default inequalities reassert themselves in various ways. And these ideals have not yet penetrated to the entirety of the world. But they embody what we might call a "loving society" on a level that goes beyond the individual.

What we are looking at is a glimpse of the kingdom of God, in which there is neither Jew nor Greek, neither slave nor free, and there is not "male and female" (Gal. 3:28). Christianity was healthy for almost two millennia without making these changes. Indeed it thrived. God was content even in the New Testament to allow the earliest believers to continue owning slaves and to continue the subordination of wives to husbands. But in these last two hundred years, God has decided not only to move the church but the world closer to the kingdom of God.

There are some crucial points of insight here. In the early 1800s in the United States, the Bible was used heavily in support of slavery. For example, in Colossians 3:22-4:1, slaves are told to obey their masters. Colossians, Ephesians, 1 Peter all assume the institution of slavery. Even a careful reading of Philemon reveals that Paul does not mention setting the slave Onesimus free.

So the "letteralists" of the early 1800s argued from the letter of Scripture that slavery should not be abolished, only reformed, and they had the letter of the Bible on their side. What they did not have was the Spirit of Scripture. Those who caught the Spirit of Scripture were groups like the Quakers and the Wesleyan Methodists. In other words, it was those with a more Pietist approach that focuses on the heart.

We are in a better position today to describe what was going on. If we listen to what the books of the Bible say about themselves, they tell us they were written to God's people two and three thousand years ago. Its original meaning has everything to do with the situations and categories of people in the ancient world. The more we know about that world, the more we recognize how well the words of the Bible connected to that world so foreign to us.

> Like Jesus and Paul, we apply Scripture rightly when we catch its Spirit and its principles rather than being "letteralists" who mistake the "that time" of Scripture with the end of time.

Groups like the Quakers and the Wesleyans, because

they focused on the big principle of loving your neighbor, were able to see beyond the ancient particulars of the Bible to the heart of the matter. Other groups, because they focused so much on the letter of the Bible, were not able to distinguish between the structures of "that time" and the trajectory of God's kingdom. So also today, the best of the Wesleyan tradition will continue to focus on changing the structures of the world following the principle of perfect love—love that extends to everyone equally.

So we are not surprised to find that the Wesleyan Methodist Church was born in 1843 over the issue of abolition. We are not surprised to find that the movement to give women the right to vote met for the first time in a Wesleyan Methodist Church in Seneca Falls, New York, in 1848. One of the founders of the Wesleyan Methodist Church preached the sermon at the first ordination of a woman minister in 1852. Long before it was trendy, the Wesleyan tradition—like the Quakers—had women pastors. They saw that the coming of the Spirit inaugurated an age when "sons and daughters will prophecy" (Acts 2:17).

The fundamental insight is this: "God shows no partiality" (Acts 10:34). He values people of all races and genders equally, and all people have equal access to the Spirit. The rest is simply playing out the principle. Wesleyans who were true to our tradition took the side of those who worked for equal rights for African-Americans in the civil rights era. Wesleyans today will recognize that God values the illegal immigrant just as much as he values me.

This spiritual insight works its way into all sorts of areas

> True Wesleyans are egalitarian in their sense of women in the church and the home, and they see people of all races and nations as equally important in God's eyes.

where a focus on the letter of the biblical text can cloud hearing the more basic Spiritual principle. For example, just as with slavery, the New Testament assumes the ancient social structure of the home, with the husband as authority and the wife as subordinate. We know it will not be that way in the kingdom. So what keeps us from enacting God's ideal now instead of waiting for the kingdom of God? Will not the best of the Wesleyan tradition follow the lead of its ancestors and see the wife as a true equal in the home?

The Wesleyan tradition will be keen to level the playing field in all areas of life. Working out the details is always complicated, and there will almost always be room for debating the best strategy or for avoiding unintended consequences. But the principles are clear. When social or economic structures put women or men at a disadvantage, when they disadvantage one people over another, the best of the Wesleyan tradition will be there to work toward the kingdom principle that God loves all people equally.

10. The Importance of Faithfulness

Protestantism was born in a debate over whether a person might gain favor with God by doing good "works." Martin Luther, of course, argued that we were saved "by grace alone" (*sola gratia*), only because of God's undeserved favor. This grace was triggered "by faith alone" (*sola fidei*), and even this faith was a gift from God. Ever since, the standard Protestant position on "faith versus works" is that we are saved by faith alone, but that once we are right with God, he will empower us so that "works" will follow.

However, Protestants have debated whether the way we live our Christian lives thereafter has an effect on our eternal destiny. Once a person has become right with God, can a person later become "un-right" with God again? To many Protestants, to say our actions can affect our status with God is tantamount to saying that works are part of our salvation. They might resolve the potential conflict by saying that if a person were to become a serial killer after "conversion," she probably had never really been a true Christian in the first place.

Jacob Arminius disagreed in the 1500 and 1600s, and John Wesley followed his lead. To some it will be a weakness, but to Wesleyans it is a

37

strength that Wesley was an Anglican, because the Anglican Church is a moderating tradition in the Catholic-Protestant debate. One might argue that Anglicanism, along with the Methodism that flowed out of it, stands on a kind of middle ground between the extremes of the Protestant Reformation, with the medieval Roman Catholic Church on the one side and the high Protestantism of Luther and Calvin on the other. The Wesleyan tradition is thus well-situated to incorporate the strengths of both Christian streams in a way many other Protestant traditions are not.

For Wesley's part, it was certainly God who empowered us to have faith. But that same empowerment to choose also enabled us to walk away from him. On the one hand, our "initial justification," our initial reconciliation to God was by faith alone, regardless of our works. To put it in current language, "all sin is sin" when we *first* come to God. But Wesley rightly read Scripture to teach that it matters how we live thereafter. God has no intention or desire to separate himself from us, but he gives us the freedom to separate from him.

We return to our orientation around the heart. Our walk with God is a relationship. In a relationship, our actions toward another person matter. Of course what matters even more is our intentions toward another. If you forget your spouse's birthday, you have "sinned" against him or her. But this "sin" is quite different from having an affair, which reflects a whole different level of intention. So also, our "works" have a varying effect on our relationship with God, depending on our heart. All sin is *not* the same after we are reconciled to him.

This understanding comes from Scripture, as we come to grips with statements like 2 Corinthians 5:10, a verse directed at Christians. "All of us must appear before the judgment seat of Christ, so that each may receive recompense for what has been done in the body, whether good or evil" (NRSV). Romans 2 says exactly the same thing: "He will repay according to each one's deeds: to those who by patiently doing good seek for glory and honor and immortality, he will give eternal life; while for those who are self-seeking and who obey not the truth but wickedness, there will be wrath and fury" (2:6-8).

And the fact that Paul himself did not consider his eternal salvation assured confirms his thinking on this subject: "I do not run aimlessly, nor do I box as though beating the air; but I punish my body and enslave it, so that after proclaiming to others I myself should not be disqualified (1 Cor. 9:26-27, NRSV). Similarly, he says in Philippians, "I want to know Christ... if somehow I may attain the resurrection from the dead. Not that I have already obtained this or have already reached the goal; but I press on to make it my own" (3:10-12).

This way of thinking fits well with the meaning of "grace" in the New Testament world. Grace was patron-client language, relating to informal arrangements where someone without resources (clients) received gifts from those having abundance (patrons). The recipient did not earn such grace, although it often came with certain expectations. We could rightly say, though, that the gift was not earned and, in a sense, came without formal obligation.

> It matters how we live after God has forgiven us of our past.

But if clients behaved badly toward the patron—if they dishonored the giver—you can rest assured that the grace would not continue. In the same way, we are not surprised that God's grace in the New Testament comes with certain expectations. Nor are we surprised to find that one can insult God's grace (e.g., Heb. 10:29) such that it is "used up," in a sense (e.g., Heb. 10:26). Hebrews, as the rest of the New Testament, places an expectation that we continue in faithfulness to reach the goal of entering the land of "Canaan." We have become partakers of Christ and remain partakers of Christ *only if* "we hold our first confidence firm to the end" (3:7, NRSV).

The point is not to raise the specter of a vindictive God. No one who loves God need ever feel insecure, even if they fail along the way. The key is the direction one is moving. It is much different to fall when walking with or toward God than to fall when walking away from him. An eternal relationship with God involves the same elements that human relationships involve. And if human relationships sometimes fail because of infidelity or neglect, we should not be surprised to find that neglect or unfaithfulness to God is a path toward separation with him as well.

11. Scripture as Sacrament

Wesleyans share with most other Christians a love for Scripture. John Wesley once described himself as "a man of one book," in reference to the Bible. At the same time, Wesley was also a student of Christian literature and did not believe that God stopped speaking to his people after the books of the New Testament were finished. Later students of Wesley have described his method of finding God's will as a "quadrilateral" consisting of Scripture, tradition, reason, and experience. Certainly in Wesley's mind Scripture had first place among these potential channels of God's voice.

This broad sense of Scripture allows the Wesleyan tradition to participate in a renewed vision today for how God works through the Bible. First and foremost, Scripture is a sacrament of transformation. It is perhaps not surprising that most of the battles over the Bible have been fought in terms of what we might call propositional truth. Does the Bible say things that are true or things that are false? Certainly this question is part of the equation, but it misses the fundamental purpose of Scripture for Christians, which is to serve as an instrument of reconciliation and transformation.

More than to reveal truth *about* God, the purpose of Christian Scripture is to *meet* God, to *encounter* God, to be changed by God. This is not to deny the legitimacy of the very complex historical method evangelical and non-evangelical scholars alike have developed over the years. You can study at an evangelical college or seminary and learn Greek, Hebrew, and Aramaic. You can learn about literary context and how to follow a train of thought. You can learn historical-cultural background in order to read the words of the Bible in context. You can learn the gamut of hermeneutical perspectives on how to integrate the varied teaching of Scripture into a biblical theology and various approaches on how to move from "that time" to "this time." Such courses of study are legitimate and will equip you to hear each book of the Bible on its own terms, the terms in which God first spoke through those words to some ancient audience.

But you may or may not be changed. For the Bible to be Christian Scripture, it must be your book. The stories that appear throughout its books must become your story. The way in which its commands, promises, teaching, and expressions become commands to you, promises to you, instruction to you, and your expressions is complex. We could go passage by passage and analyze the complex ways in which not only common Christianity but specific denominations and individuals have experienced God appropriating these words for them. No doubt at times they have heard him wrongly. Arguably this is why there was a Protestant Reformation.

But appropriating Scripture is surely a

> The Bible is a sacrament of transformation, and its appropriation is ultimately a spiritual task.

spiritual task, another point where the Wesleyan tradition, along with its sister Pentecostal traditions, potentially has something to contribute. Many other Christian traditions, in combating modernism, too quickly adopted its categories. The Protestant Reformation also, in its reaction to medieval Catholicism, perhaps too quickly rejected the possibility that the Spirit might speak beyond the "literal" meaning of the Bible. In doing so, it seems to have missed the fact that the New Testament itself frequently reads the Old Testament in this sort of "spiritual" way.

As the Wesleyan tradition moves forward into the twenty-first century, it along with other like-minded traditions can suggest we begin to take a more "sacramental" and less mechanistic view of Scripture. A sacrament is a divinely appointed means of God's grace, where God takes something that is ordinary—like bread or water—and meets us in an extraordinary way in it. Is not the Bible like that? These are ordinary words. Indeed, they employ the categories and common language of the people to whom they were first written.

But the Bible is a special place to meet God and be transformed into his likeness both as individuals and as communities of faith. Certainly it is a sacrament of revelation through which our thinking and understanding of truth is transformed to be sure. We will want to study it for what it really meant, God's first moment of speaking through it. But even after we have done all our homework, after we have done our best to understand its words in context, appropriating those words for today is a spiritual task. Even more, it is a corporate task, for I am surely even more likely to know the Spirit's leading in a community of Spirit-filled individuals than I am alone.

But as much as it is a place to meet God with my mind, it is even more a place for my heart and my actions to be changed. It is a place for me to see myself in the stories and words and for us corporately to see ourselves. It is a place for me to recognize the path I must take and the path we must take together. God's leading through Scripture is not something we can set down in a formula or even a creed, although creeds rightly capture the corporate sense God has given Christians of the boundaries. It is a spiritual leading that defies our desire for tidy answers and absolute clarity.

Wesley set a great precedent here for the Wesleyan tradition and beyond. He began with Scripture, as we all should. But because he lived in the eighteenth century, he had a certain kind of freedom to read and connect the Scriptures to one another in a spiritual rather than mechanistic, historical way. He drank deeply from the writings of Christians throughout the centuries, which gave him illumination that the Spirit had brought to Christians throughout the centuries, as well as the boundaries within which the Spirit moves. But he was also open to experiencing the Spirit freshly through the words of the Bible and to receiving specific guidance for our lives from them.

Scripture for him was about God changing us, about God moving us along on the path of salvation.

12. Looking Ahead

The Wesleyan tradition, like all Christian traditions, has its strengths and no doubt its weaknesses. Its greatest strengths are no doubt those elements it shares in common with all other Christians today and throughout the ages. Nevertheless, just perhaps, it has some distinctive strengths that enrich the body of Christ. May God give us the vision to contribute in these ways to the church universal! If we have the will, he has the power.

[1] Cf. Robert Black and Keith Drury, *The Story of the Wesleyan Church* (Indianapolis: Wesleyan Publishing, 2012), 37.

[2] The idea of us being judged according to the light we have was frequently held by members of the Pilgrim Holiness Church, one of the parents to the Wesleyan Church to which I belong, no doubt in part because of the Quaker influence on that tradition. In general, the idea that the majority of people who have lived on the planet will go to hell because they haven't heard seems inconsonant with Wesleyan theology, although it fits well with Calvinist theology.

[3] An excellent book from the Wesleyan tradition to push back on the insistence on penal substitution in some evangelical circles is *Rediscovering the Scandal of the Cross: Atonement in New Testament and Contemporary Contexts* (Downers Grove, IL: InterVarsity, 2000).

[4] In fact, to equate "evangelism" with "getting people saved" is a drastically incorrect sense of the gospel. The gospel in the New Testament was the good news that God's reign was returning to the world and that Jesus is God's enthroned king over the whole universe. One of the implications of that good news is that we can escape God's coming judgment on the world, but it is only one implication. Indeed, for the Gospel of Luke the good news is much more good news for the poor and freedom for those oppressed (Luke 4:18).

Made in the USA
Lexington, KY
05 October 2012